THE CHARGE

THE CHARGE

Patrick Donnelly

AUSABLE PRESS
2003

Cover art: Gandee Vasan /Getty Images.
Design and composition by Ausable Press.
The type is Centaur.
Cover design by Rebecca Soderholm.

Published by
AUSABLE PRESS
1026 HURRICANE ROAD
KEENE NY 12942-9712
www.ausablepress.com

Distributed by
SMALL PRESS DISTRIBUTION
800-869-7553
www.spdbooks.org

The acknowledgments appear on page 81 and constitute
a continuation of the copyrights page.

Library of Congress Cataloging-in-Publication Data
Donnelly, Patrick, 1956–
The charge : poems / by Patrick Donnelly.
p. cm.
ISBN 1-931337-15-2 (hardcover : alk. paper)
ISBN 1-931337-16-0 (pbk. : alk. paper)
I. Title.
PS3604.O6356C47 2003
813'.6–dc22
2003015472

for Cliff
who helped me learn
for Dinah
who helped me live
for Martha
who helped and helped

THE CHARGE

I

HOW IS IT SOMETIMES

How is it sometimes a black shape,
as this morning a brisk shadow
shouldered by me to the street
out of the dark arcades under the city,
his hair—I knew it was a he—
cut close like a cap, a glimpse
of narrow hips under a blurred coat or cape—
a sketch, the bare suggestion of a face,
of fine eyes, luster, pallor—
this little, flashing past
and already lost, is enough to leave
an impression of handsomeness?
Strange but already cherished silhouette—
rushing, peripheral—to what image
do you correspond behind my eye,
in my brain or starveling heart, and who
engraved the outline of longing there?

Every day I risk more danger—daring
to turn full face and look at the sun
rising over my shoulder's cold earth—
never disappointed, in the instant before
blindness and ash, beauty always confirmed,
sometimes—oh, luminous!—even looking back.

YOUR OWN STONE

If you're smart, before you cook,
you'll sort black beans on a white plate
and pick out the stones. If you miss
a small, porous bead, like the cliffs of tufa
in which old Indians scratched their caves,
it might dissolve in your stew
and add some positive minerals,
but a hard boil means nothing
to a dense little stone.

It may get into the bag on the table
by the hand of a peasant, that pebble,
or the hand of a child of a peasant,
from the scrabble of some high
and loveless field where there's nothing
but rocks to eat,
                    like the rock
that got into my mouth,
the stone my father sent me.
My father gave me a stone
and I ate it.

PRAYER AT THE OPERA

I had already been weeping quietly
for half an hour at the Academy of Music
by the time Ulysses finally made it home
disguised as a beggar. He was begging
for his son to recognize him, to *know* him,
and the boy longed to, but a whole kingdom
hung on this, and he was afraid to love a fraud.

When the Croatian baritone
stretched out his hand to the boy,
quivering thin and lonely
on the other side of the stage,
and sung his name softly,
Telemaco, Telemaco, mio diletto,
it was as if the floor of the world
tilted the boy into his arms,

and because I thought I heard my father calling,
I thought all voices were my voice begging
You, who made it easy for me to weep:
lend the gift of tears
to a man my mother said cried two times,
when Kennedy was shot,
and at my birth.

THE PRODIGAL SON

When did Jesus-son-of-Joseph work his craft,
I want to know? When did he worry songs
into a shape, spit into the dirt and scribble,
fiddle sawdust into parabolic piles,
count beats on his peaceful toes?
Publish this Word! and let me worship it,
for the miracle of thrift, where one detail
pulls all the others onto the painted scene:
While he was yet a great way off
his father saw him
and ran,
and fell on his neck,
and kissed him.
From these few words
we know the father watched the high road every day,
watched and misadded the long figures of the year,
watched and manured the strawberries,
watched and beat the blameless servants.
And every day shapeless blots crossed the horizon,
and every night camels, and other people's sons,
and every month the farm ran better
and made more useless money,
until finally the stupid pressure of longing
wrenched one personal smudge off the vista,
and dragged it up the steep incline to the house,
where it took the shape of what he lost

and shoved blood out of his heart like a death—

The servant was chasing fallen leases, invoices,
return authorizations
across the flagstones of the porch,
and the father found himself running
toward the poor shape, stuck in the far dirt
to rehearse its little speech—
running to that sweet neck
like a deer to the smell of apples.

AN EARFUL

He's carrying a large watermelon home
from the cooperative in a mesh bag.
Carrying a watermelon,
say two girls with lots of red lipstick
who giggle and jab each other,
look back to see if he's heard.

*

After a massage, relaxed and smelling of rose oil,
he walks with strangers past a drunk,
who scrunches up his nose:
One of you is wearing too much perfume.

*

His hand is on his big straw hat
on a hot breezy day, when an old lady
crosses the avenue against him:
Wrong day for a hat like that.

*

Three little black boys call out
where they dance in the hydrant spray:
Are you gay?

Chasing after him
areyougay areyougay
Blocks away their cries like wild birds
areyougay areyougay areyougay

*

He's cutting fresh coriander, and out
the summer window light rain
makes yarrow bend into the dirt.

Wind chimes, thunder, dog-bark.

Neighbor's voice, tired and soft:
Yeah, bark at God,
see where that gets you.

HIS *CAFÉ CON LECHE* HANDS

Immaculate white apron, tied low
around his supple Little Cuba hips,
like the Guadalupe over the counter
without stain or spot of any kind
(though God knows I long to spill
something of myself across that almost-altar,
stumble into the snowfield of his sheets)—
he glitters like an otter
doing the forbidden *lambada*,
and oh, the little shake
he always gives my iced hazelnut
to mix it with heavy cream
(sweet whiteness falling, tumbling
through dark, bitter body),
before I pierce the little pucker
with my straw,
my mighty, mighty straw!

PRAYER AFTER THE BATHS

Thank You
for causing no man to love me
for more than a few minutes at a time
with such art as big, tall Tom has used this night,

because when he took off his baseball cap
to rub his buzzcut along my belly,
murmuring under his breath a baritonal "Sweet,"
I was in danger of becoming one of those
who have their reward in *this* life,

and then the proud palm-shaded pew
You in Your famous jealousy
have prepared for me
among the ranks of minor martyrs
might have gone
unoccupied.

YOUNG MAN READING COLETTE ON THE TRAIN

You hold my gaze a little too long,
your hair cut short like a boy's,
your fine little glasses,
at your ear, glint of gold,
in your cheek, a slight shade of wasting:
This is to say I see you, I know you,
I am alert to your potential, to ours,
on this train, on every train,
on the platform, on the stairs to the street,
on the dim threshold, in the elevator
stopped between floors, in its flickering lights,
then in that dark opening, if we are spared,
where I may find my way
to you, graceful ghost of a chance.

SWEET FOR ALL SOULS'

His huge mother sweats,
turns to count my change,
slowly, *slowly,* breathing hard
as she rolls her chair to the register
behind the scratched glass counter.
The smell of burning sugar
vents from ovens in back,
over me, out to the street
where they are hanging lights
for the festival, and where,
in the middle of my life,
in Brooklyn, in autumn,
in the afternoon of the century,
some poor soul has scribbled
thick, black magicmarkings:
"SICK OF IT ALL."
Sick, really? of everything?
Of *ossi di morti,* these yearly
bones of the sacred dead
turned to sweet meringues
you can pop in your mouth?
Sick of Ettore, the baker's son, just today
sixteen in baseball cap and baggy shorts,
blond feather on his lip, brick
of Tuscan gold from tip to toe?
who assembles my box from nothing,
knots the string and clips it

with hands of such deft and clever caramel?
who once washed his car in the street,
shirtless chest bright as the resurrection?
The little sweets in his hands
shake the thrones of the saints,
they enlarge my heart—

this sickness is my master,
I groan on his bed,
I swell and fall,
I never rise

BABA

Baba feeds me with his own hand:
the night my friend died
he pressed dark chocolate
into a macaroon, and the sweetness
cut the pain; another time
he showed me how to fry
black mustard seed in ghee,
spooned silky dhal between my lips
with one raised eyebrow:
"Enough salt? Enough cumin?"
The day he gave me his hand
Baba wore a robe the color of mint.
Sometimes he ignores me for weeks,
then comes to me in dreams
riding a tractor or sitting on a deerskin.

Baba has three small moles
on the left side of his face.
When he prays, we see
the bottom of his socks are dirty.
He plays a blues lick on his '66 Fender;
in the dark his glasses glint and hide his eyes.
He says if you're very quiet
you can hear a sound inside
like crickets singing, then sleeps
with his head in my lap.
Baba shouts at us to stay awake,

says we can sleep when we're dead,
he rocks back and forth when he chants,
sends his wives around
to splash us with rosewater.
Baba gives me his hats
he moves sick people away from me
he drives a red pickup
he gave me five hundred dollars
he gave me a new name.

Baba disappears into a photo booth at the airport,
reappears to give me
a small version of his face.
He cut all his hair off, then he grew it again,
he wears no coat when it's cold.
Baba passes me in the coffeehouse, writes
"beh-sin-mim-alif-lam-lam-ha"
at the top of my letter, *Bismillah,* since
Baba does everything in God's name.
When he rolls a smoke
on a picnic table in the moonlight,
watching trains go from Chicago
to New Orleans and back again,
a circle always gathers
to ask the hard questions:
what about abortion, what about gay people,
what happens when you die?

In the silence before he answers
I know the stories about Jesus are true:

but Baba, Baba, I can hardly keep up—
my heart runs after you
with my soul in its hands.

ANGEL'S TRUMPET

In order to tell him he would die
a few weeks shy of 28, I needed only
to place two vials of brown glass
on the bedside table, in front of his tissues and tulips.

"Which are they?" he asked.

"Angelica," I said first, reading from the book,
"angelica archangelica,
protection of the angelic realm."

Then the other (almost casually),
"datura candida, Angel's Trumpet," and did not read
"for when the soul must utterly surrender."

It was not my place, was it?—
to put the cold embouchure to my lips
and blow.

POOL

The fat man with purple sores all over his legs
is looking at me, and I am elaborately
not looking at him, as we wait for children
to clear the pool and laps to begin.
Shall I call the lifeguard? *I'm afraid*
of the fat man with his almost-open sores
I don't tell her, and I don't ask what it will mean
to climb into the pool with him, because no one can say,
and when I lay my body into the slow lane alongside his,
where he can't keep from brushing, from touching me
as we roll to breathe, at the end of every lap
he is waiting, he is watching, he is looking at me.

WHITE SHIRT

Nothing the poet at the podium has read
is as achieved as his shirt, which is white,
so white a white its very shadows are Antarctic,
a pronouncement of magnificent power,
able to make immaculate
a few yards of cloth in this dirty world,
if only for a morning, before he sweats at the pits
and drags the cuffs through his lunch.

It took an army to keep the Virgin Queen's satin clean,
and the man who invented the starch
that kept the court's ruffs stiff and bright
got a knighthood and fortune:
we work to keep an area of the world
clear around our faces and necks,
so we can be seen in the right light, so we can breathe.

But *The Road to Perdition* shows
a man lured laughing and drunk
by whores through a red-lit door—
not even the main character, this poor jerk,
just some peripheral guy who doesn't know
the only way to be free is not to need
what's through that door.
                              No dirt can touch the few
who are clean that way, but for the rest of us,
as amply proved by luminous frogs

in a mural on my block,
over whose delicate spatulate toes
someone has spray-painted FUCK FUCK FUCK:

there is no way in the world to keep pure.

FINDING PAUL MONETTE,
LOSING HIM

It's just two days since I read you
two days since your *Elegies for Rog* grabbed me
in the stacks at the Brooklyn branch
grief eating through the binding like dragon blood
dripping through four stone floors
into the charming restaurant in the basement
I checked you out and brought you home
so I could love you and pity him in private
and cry for him and you and myself
I never burned up grief or anger with such song
never came within two bow-lengths of the paradise
of men's hearts open to one another
I'll check you out again and again
I think I'll steal you
I don't want to release you back to circulation
I study your picture on the sleeve for signs of sickness
search the flyleaf for year of publication
could you have survived 1987
so long ago dangerous year
to be a sick fag in America
In the cafe at the gay bookstore
I'm afraid to ask Do you know Monette
Did he make it The boys are so young
thumbing through pages of naked men
putting them back dogeared The boy
behind the counter doesn't read poetry

I'm afraid of hope as I walk
to the back of the store PLEASE BE ALIVE
PLEASE BE among the M's I run my hand
along the spines Maupin McClatchy Melville
until it rests on yours
I tear you open the suspense killing me
please *please* be living with the dogs
in the canyons somewhere north of Malibu
writing every day doing well on the new drugs
sleeping like spoons with a guy named
Peter Kenneth Michael or Gustavo
Your picture is harder thinner
face lined eyelids sagging "novelist poet essayist
AIDS activist who died"
                                        You're gone then
I've made it to the future a few years further
but who knows if I'll reach your forty-nine
why bother reading your book anymore
what difference do poems make or love
So this is your last face a fox and rabbit kissing
even dead your name earns a "face-out"
guarantees those big sales
who gets the money now
YOU JERK FUCK YOU
ridiculous to die so close to a cure
renders you me us absurd
shameful irresponsible

how quaint to die of this they'll think in 2030
how nostalgically sepia-toned and old-timey
like dying of the flu for godssake or the clap
like talking on a windup telephone or
buying ice for the icebox
                              On the Net later
I cruise a guy who says he knew you
when you tried to live and love again with Winston
I'm hungry to hear anything about you
but he interrupts with a reflection of his cock
in a hand mirror in a garden of red hibiscus
so for a moment I almost easily forget my love
my love of two days
two days in which you were born loved wrote grieved
        died

Oh God in whom you never for one moment believed
will I still have time

BUS STATION, NEW MEXICO

"The bus is leaving
without you," a voice warns,
but I'm lost, wondering
where I might find him,
the blond boy with gray gloves
the poster says is missing.

II

PRAYER AFTER REFUSING TO PRAY

Why, when the ferocious beauty that steers this world
has never braked for any cry of mine,

do I find myself making again, toward You
who will always do just as You please,

these motions with my lips and hands and knees,
trying to gentle Your vast wheel off the rails?

My friend is sick in the lymph behind his heart,
a monk, a teacher, Your servant, who loved You so.

RUNE FOR MICHAEL,
SICK AND FAR AWAY

The needle and the pill with all their smartness,
the churches with their darkness, and their loud alarms,
the scriptures, and Christ's crossed body, and every holy thing,
my kitchen with its pies and kettles, and my knowledge
of how to knot ties and drive cars with gears,
my garden and the strength of all its weeds and seeds,
their power to appear again,
the phone with its extension and its electric leaping,
my voice, and the warm blood in it,
my singing, with its proud health and sweet connectedness,
the wings of my imagined self, and my best silver,
my eyes with their blindness of what might come,
my tallness that sees over things,
my thinness that fills a crack of God,
my memory, my promise, my written name—

may the power in these charms be enough.

RIDDLE

What can't be seen,
     but strikes you blind?
What doesn't breathe,
     but takes your breath away?
What can't be touched,
     but will be felt?
What travels with love,
     but is hated?
What never eats,
     but consumes?
What doesn't grow, but increases?
     Isn't alive, but kills?
What is no animal, vegetable, or mineral,
     has no king or kingdom?
What came from nowhere?
     What is everywhere?
What makes your cells its brothel,
     your life, its toilet?
What? What? What?

CONSUMMATUM EST

With the certainty theologians claim
for the salvation worked by Christ—
effects not yet seen,
but the end not in doubt—
some women look back and know
the exact moment they conceived.

He brought me home from the baths
and fed me takeout Chinese. I remember
succulent little bits of egg in rice,
creamy sherbet right out of the carton.
Yes—certainly I felt it—and broke
into a sweat, the exact moment
the charge leapt from him to me.

Was it two years later his best friend called—
could I use his clothes, his shoes, his king-size bed?

THE SIGN AT WINDOW ONE

reads: THE CLOCK IS TICKING.

What brings my red Irish face
among the blackest of black faces, crêpe to crow,
applicants waiting in lines that snake to the street,
even the guards and low-level functionaries
one paycheck from the street themselves,
who move languidly from office to office,
or hunch, two or three at a time, bickering
over a task that might well be done by one;
among a caste of voices, Billie-Holiday-hoarse,
of bored kids sucking on empty starches;
among the missing teeth and big earrings of poverty
at a Brooklyn welfare office—sorry, "job center"—
in mudtracked midwinter?

I check the box that says "sex with men"as the reason
I was infected; the reason I am here to hear,
from one cubicle over, a voice that asks:

Any changes, my brother?

HARM REDUCTION

An old grandfather with half-closed eyes and yellow beard
slumps early with drink on the steps of my clinic,
acting out his affliction under a marble arch.

Every excess leaves a scar—

If only he had chosen love for his addiction,
he might have drunk that cup to its secret,
sweet, muddy dregs again and again,
and kept his dignity before these passersby,
as I do, for a time.

SACRAL

I creep east along Twenty-third Street, crooning to the wound
the surgeon made, horizontal cut just above my right thigh,
another swollen node removed, lesion in my sacral chakra,
seat of sex and grasping, everything base and low.
And here I've come to the Chelsea Hotel, its beautiful balconies,
dead now, everyone who lived there:
Dylan Thomas, Thomas Wolfe, Virgil Thompson;
the self-destructive, the sarcastic, the charming;
the late James Ingram McCarthy, all of these,
my first New York love,
first to exchange his beauty for a respirator,
first person to die while I was still mad at him;
and Curtis too is gone, who was a Quaker,
who drank cheap wine from a coffee cup,
who could lift me over his head, who gave me the clap (twice);

and Diego is dead,
who brought me away from the Adonis in a cab,
away from men leaning over the balustrade of the oval oculus,
disappearing in pairs into the dark niches
between the urns of dusty lilacs;
who made me tunafish sandwiches in the middle of the night;
who slept through lightning striking the building next door;
who was too Latin to let any insult slide, especially the word *fag*,
who smashed a bottle against a wall and gave chase to the thugs
        that spoke it,
who paid with bruises, ribs broken and taped,

who wanted to make love anyway only two days after,
who was too Latin to lie back and let me do the work of it—
who couldn't wait, who had to have it—
fucking like poisonous starfish or porcupines—
who finally crumpled with pain, with laughing, hankering and
        pain;
whose head in his last days I held, whose deaf ear I told *You can*
        make it,
then rinsed danger off my hands at the little hospital sink,
as I had after fetching poison from the basement as a child.

Dear Diego, which Greek was it, the hero with a wound
that stank to high heaven and would not heal?

PRAYER AT THE GYM

Only an All-Powerful Name
invoked again and again
gives me victory
over middle age, a chronic virus,
the disinclination to lift these weights,
and the crevice between my eyes
reflected to me from mirrors that are everywhere
mocking the idea that my body can be beautiful in this life.

But I'm shocked to discover,
looking up from my hundredth whispered *Bismillah,*
I'm not the only one praying here:
the brute on the fly machine
with the black bandana over his shaved skull—
R. I. P. WOLFMAN SHORTY inked by hand
on his right biceps, Twin Towers on the left,
his sexy little belly, if I read right, that says
he's caught the kitty too (from shooting up,
my guess, and not like me, from men)—
as he inserts the weight pin at 150
murmurs "Just one more,"
crosses himself, kisses
something he holds in his right hand,
then touches the weights in front of his heart
with a tremendous spasm of will—

    Oh God

help us to lift it
and go on lifting it,
the heavy burden of Your light.

PRAYER OVER A BOX OF BOOKS

Books in a box marked FREE
on a Brooklyn stoop; last chance for them
to suggest their narrative about a dancer
who came to New York City by September 14, 1982,
as a receipt shows, inside the cover
of *La Danse Artistique aux États-Unis.*

It seems he found here *The Culture of Desire,*
fell in love with *The Front Runner* and *The Persian Boy,*
drank *The Last of the Wine,*
and got sober with the *Big Book,* or tried.

But does the hardcover *How We Die*
come before or after *The Suicidal Patient?*
Did he find what he searched for
in *Tales of the Hasidim* or *The Last of the Just?*
At what moment was Paradise lost for good and for all?

And had it belonged to the one behind the drawn blind
who put the box this morning at the foot of the stoop,
the copy of *Caregiving in a Time of AIDS,*
or was it my dancer's, and had he also known
what it was like to put out a box like this?

This is how we live now:
the light going out
in one pair of eyes after another.

APOLOGIA PRO VITA SUA

A year after his mother handed me the cardboard box
that held his mind with a few of his other things,
I put the crashed computer on the sidewalk.
It's someone else's turn to put it to use.
Let them read his tender, hidden thoughts,
and my later ones, lodged beside in memory.
                                        I don't care:
I lived this way, the windows open wide,
in summer the doors, anyone passing could see
and take what they wanted, and they did.

CONJUREMENT

A week before the lease was finished
and I had to leave that place, iris and lilac
exhaled urgent freshness over the yard, breathing
from purple tissue so tender as to be torn
by sunlight. In the morning a moon hung
at the end of every street, testing the limit
of fullness, soon to be empty,

and in the afternoon I watched David
pull back a corner of John's hospital gown,
to put a hand over his heart,
careful not to dislodge tubes and catheters,
at first just resting, then giving his nipple
a light, almost furtive tickle: final appeal
to the secret mercy of pleasure,
that terrible god.

III

NOTE TO THE NEW OWNER

Because you toured the house with the termite inspector,
baby in your arms, your mother in tow, then out the door
without speaking to me—to me! who had watched my face
age twelve years in these mirrors—I determined

to root every living thing out of the garden—*my* garden,
that I created *ex nihilo*, that I nursed in sour shade
between shards of broken glass, that I made and now revoke,
breaking every bleeding heart and fiddleneck.

Your mother gasped with delight at forced branches
flowering in a glass bowl in the kitchen. She, at least, is a person.
For her sake I leave the forsythia to explode each spring.

AFTER A MOVE

These are not my keys,
this is not my door.
I'm so tired, I could sleep anyplace,
but this is not my bed.
This is not my street,
not my face,
not my dirt
where someone's hand
touched the wall again and again
to help themselves down the stairs.
These are not my eyes,
not my leaves, not my light,
nothing like the view I knew.
These words are not mine,
none of this food is mine,
and when I asked for the kind of sandwich I like
the man behind the counter said nothing but:
No.

FOUNTAIN OF BLOOD

Les grands jets d'eau sveltes parmi les marbres

Sometime last week, in my neighbor's yard,
whoever it was, with whatever tool, broke up the concrete,
arranged the shattered slag around an oval of soil
that last looked at light and drank rain circa 1894,
and plunged a plant into that barely-breathing dirt.

I hate to say just *plant*, I've known men and women less alive
than this ornamental grass—"ornamental" a slander
unless a tiger is an ornament, a leaping zebra,
a striped fountain of blood, a great grass-gush seven feet tall
jetting panicles like foxtails over the fence, soft to the touch,
weeping rye, oats, millet, wheat, bread and the broken host of
       love
to the pavement, to be licked up by deertongue
and the ghosts of our long lost Brooklyn sheep and stock.

How will it live, in these ruins? How will I?

MY SIDE OF THE WALL

My neighbors' bitch in rut
behind the wall we share:
all night the moans and gasps God-bitten
dervishes use in prayer.

I can't complain to her owners
because of cries *they* hear
when loneliness lures some kind of love
to my solitary lair.

HARD GARDENS

In October, three postcards come
from wandering friends:
a cottage on a cliff, with hollyhocks
leaning over the sea;
fat beds of lavender
resuscitated at Giverny;
the brief bluebell wood
at Brooklyn Botanic.

Why do they put these gardens upon me?
I've got no lease to these rooms,
I'm too old, it's too late,
winter is coming . . .

and the White Garden
at Sissinghurst,
the pleasure house
where I sucked on a joint
and watched the moon rise—
that whole glory-book,
its shimmer, is shut.

LOW DOOR

I must become very modest,
flexible, small and sweet to enter here,
at six-foot-six, me,
to have such a door,
to inhabit a hobbit-hole,
an "English Basement"
down three steps with a twist
under a Brooklyn stoop;
to bend in half
like a Muslim at prayer
to fit the brass, then the silver key,
knapsack sliding off my shoulder,
bicycle helmet crashing against the lintel,
to genuflect into the tiny vestibule,
to find by feel alone, in the dark,
by its sloping shoulders, the gold key
to another, still smaller, door;
every night in winter
to open that door to warmth,
always a surprise—oil delivered,
furnace chanting the beautiful names,
heat circulating—
none of it my doing;
to fall into full prostration of amazement
to have a house at all,
to have a body and be alive
to live in it.

PSALM FOR MOVING DAY

Serve the Lord with horseradish
and eat like those who are on standby.

Serve the tenant with a subpoena
and drive him from the house
with flaming headaches.

For great is the tilt of the lintel
and the slant of the floor.

Stove and fridge vibrate the Landlord;
heat and dissolve Him forever.

He will raise up a new house
on the third day. Or fourth.

Let the homeless call out on Wednesdays
with a loud Voice.

Let the new house open its mouth and say *Ah.*

Let the old fairies wait with their blessings
until it is almost too late.

Let the rent go to the Landlord
on the first without fail;

Let the envelope have a window
so the checks may see out.

Let the night have a door
so the cars may have privacy.

Let the stainless not lie with the silver,
and let them have separate mouths.

Rejoice with an Actuary
who turns the gas on and off at will.

Praise with exposed brick,
rising like a wall.

Come forth with a cell phone,
that I may move and shake at the same time.

Come forth with a broom and cleanse the new house
of cat piss and hypodermic needles.

Come forth with rented emeralds
that I may go among café society.

And let there be a bridegroom,
and let him have a car,
and let him come from New Jersey.

And let light find its way
through the windows by day,
and the sweet air all night,
but no manner of unidentified youths,
for the length of the lease, amen.

TO A VARIEGATED BEGONIA

This is your best incarnation.
Finally on the *piano nobile* of a Brooklyn brownstone,
your star-shaped leaves and blood-red stems
flood with sun every morning at six;
your roots test security
in earthenware I found on the street
that still smells strongly of someone else's rosemary.
All those years we spent in the English Basement,
with its floods and mice and molds and neighbors
who seemed to stomp deliberately on the floor, are over.

But I don't know if you are the same you
I stole twenty years ago from an apartment I cleaned,
just as I'm not sure I am the same I
who carried a slip of you home on the subway in a jar
with a little wet paper towel, or the same I
who left you in a dish of water for weeks at a time,
who couldn't live my life to suit a plant goddammit,
who plunged out the door again and again
on a pilgrimage to the Bronx, California, Amsterdam,
to cast my seed among stones and weeds.

AFTER A LONG TIME AWAY

Everything is glad of me.
The radio plays only flutes.
My key fits locks all over town,
turns them over and over,
churches open their double doors,
the library has stacked all the books
in my favorite order. My throat
starts singing up and up.
Plants think up fresh leaves,
even the dust on the shelves
has got a new pair of shoes,
and waxy yellow peppers jump in my pots,
cook cheaply into a thick glee.
Trucks kindly do not grind my house apart;
the checks I write clear quietly and completely
in and out of the twilight, water-cool
vaults of my blue marble bank.
And death is just a word,
like *doorjamb, magpie,*
that twirls and worries gently.

IV

I AM SLEEPING WHERE YOU DIED

The days are short,
the trees bare
again like then.
The scar of your departure
down the narrow stair
still arcs the wall.

Oh my little friend—

thank you for the hollow
you left in this pillow.
I practice
putting my bones here.

THE SECOND GOING

My first death I acted in a play,
hoping my false hair would stick till the curtain,
trying to breathe invisibly and squint
past my eyelashes up to the deep fly,
up to dusty drops the Masons hung
to decorate their ascent by weird degrees.
I could make out a forest, a grotto,
a palace where peacocks shrieked
in the moonlight. It was a relief
after so much fencing with dull foils
to rest and hear voices resolving conflict
from a distance, the last little bits of dialogue;
to listen for the calls and applause
that would raise me up like Lazarus,
twenty nights, until the show went dark.

This was years before the twenty nights and days
I watched at your bedside,
wiped cold sweat off your neck,
lifted your head to take a drink,
looked hard at how the thing was done.

Now when my real time comes, dear critic,
I'll tune every gesture as you taught,
the thousand small details of my performance
instinct with life itself—
there! you'll cry, *that dying fall,*
an artist in every cell.

LAST WATCH

Without my knowing, the clasp opened
on the subway platform, a clatter on the tiles
I only hear in retrospect, and now
someone else must be enjoying
my watch with its Navajo turquoise,
much admired by friends,
by my doctor of ten years,
who is ill himself now, and takes no calls.

Was it trying to escape, all along?
It went through the wash twice;
had to be fitted with new hands,
which kept coming unstuck.
And once, from a nightstand,
leapt out an attic dormer and lay with leaves
in the gutter for days, till painters found it.
Or was it struggling to stay, but finally unable?

Where the watch used to be, my wrist is pale,
my pulse flooding and scattered.
This is how the dictionary defines *caducous:*
"deciduous, as of leaves, dropping off very early,
subject to shedding, destined to fall."

SHADE GARDEN

The tree of heaven in my neighbor's yard
is blocking the light in mine.

Five years ago tomatoes flourished,
sunflowers; now moss

infects flagstone, feral violets
hunch beneath nettle,

morning glory
turns its face away.

But if the sun doesn't rise, and rain
whips the ferns till they break,

tomorrow will be mushrooms,
beige and round, like the Chinese pills

I began this week.
One can garden the shade,

can kneel at night with a spade
and beg bleeding heart

to shake its wand
of lucky silver teeth.

PRAYER AT THE HOSPITAL

Forty-three and three days comatose
when the choir he had conducted paid a visit,
could John hear it when a stout contralto
stepped to his bed—but not too close—
to misquote Browning with conviction?
("John, The Best Is Yet To Come.")
Was it a struggle to wake himself
and correct their pitch
with his usual cheerful sarcasm,
or a darker impulse, that crossed his face
when Our Lady's nervous octet
surrounded his bed and shouted
an impressive arrangement
of *Jesus Christ Is Risen Today,*
while David, John's ten-year live-in love,
a nonobservant Jew, looked on,
a little apart and quiet?

     Dear Jesus,
subtle rabbi of Nazareth—who never, either,
mastered the knack of growing old—
come quickly, collect your flock,
and teach them—can you?—
not to burden the last of life
with thick and graceless certainty.

BEAUTIFUL ORPHANS

A crutch in the trash:
the age of miracles is not past.

I took you piece by piece,
checked your organs
off my list: mine, mine, mine.

A slip of garlic skin
rocks in the spider web:
an animal
has caught
a plant.

The "Neighborhood Watch" sign
with its single all-seeing eye, is bent,
hangs by one screw—

My garbageman wears a diamond in his ear.

A slab of bluestone leans in my neighbor's yard.
His kids chalked a puppy, a moon, a bird;
rain washed them away.

I turn the comforter with the roses upside down.
No one will see them,
I need them next to my body.

My neighbor—
how does he sleep, I wonder,
while his doorbell glows?

NOW HE

Now he's painting watercolors
from a saucer in the coffeehouse,
now he's about twenty
with a face clean as honey,
now he's tilting the little shade
to get more light,
concentrating, dipping
into the water mug, dabbing
with a tissue, knuckles shining,
sketching air parabolas
with the wrong end of his brush,
guinea-tee scalloping his white throat—
now I wish you would drop that brush
and catch me
loving you—
before the fan sucks me out
with the smoke.

SOTTO VOCE

My lunch break over in the Greek diner
(the spinning case of cakes,
the blue and white paper cups
with the Greek key around the lip),
the young cashier with an old-fashioned hearing aid
returns my hello in a reedy, pressed voice
that holds a history
of never quite having heard itself,
but somehow she segues without a breath
into singing along with the loud, sad song
on the radio: *You're my angel*, she sings,
cupping my hand from underneath
as she drops silver into it.

PRAYER ON THE WAY TO AN MRI

O Lord, thou hast searched me, and known me. —*Psalm 139*

How lucky to have a seat on this train,
so comfort spreads a flush of generosity
over everything: over the young man
with a paper poppy on his lapel
(in sympathy with something),
over the paraplegic child staring dumbfounded
at the ceiling above his special stroller,
and the dark lady who tucks his blanket,
over the overwhelming smell
of soap and sleep and morning,
over even my distressing desire
to know or to be the man
with beautiful feet in sandals
who steps among the wingtipped and pinstriped
wearing his casual handsomeness
like the skin of a deer.

At every stop, the doors pull apart
to reveal people hesitating shyly,
as if they need to understand
and approve the goings-on inside
before committing to anything rash.
Get on, get on! I think at them,
it's safe today, everything we've done
weighed on the tenderest of scales—

and You, who scent the air

with the unmistakable pressure of Your presence,
who probe me,
before whose invisible, amorous eye
the shy universe can't help but unbolt her door—

remember Your mercy when, a little later,
You tell me where there's wickedness in me.

MALEDICTION ON AN IRON BED

How can I curse the crook who crept through my broken bed-
    room window,
leaving his blood on the sill, burgling my computer, the delicate
    shell
that sat so many hours on my lap, magic lantern and tabernacle,
and all my work inside it, out the window,

when, a month before, I had burgled myself worse,
letting a suave Brooklyn bravo penetrate my little budget of
    health
to hear him call me puppy and his angel—oh yes, for an hour
of pretend love I let that adorable thug pry apart with a bloody,
    septic bone
the expensive cells, vessels, organelles that formed those words.

PRAYER OVER DUST

Into the kitchen bucket
go the bitter carrot tops,
collard ribs, burned heels,
drain-catcher leavings, useless
skins of things or their stringy hearts.

To these I've begun to add
my nail clippings and clumps
of hair that catch in the brush,
a way my mind chooses
to practice a hard thing.

But my body has lost interest
in the distinction between
Me and Not Me, rushes ahead
to the black box in the yard
with the mail-order worms:
fungus rings germinate
in my dark, moist places,
rash flashes up my torso,
my tongue wears white scum
and a sour, clabbered smell.

You, who cause the chemistry
of things coming apart
to give off an almost social warmth—
when it's over, let my body

be useful, let little bears
nose through my guts
for grubs, let Destroying Angel
lift its wild orchid umbrella
where my heart used to be.

PROJECTION

This flashing creature, my niece, dives to the blue bottom
to fetch something I've thrown there.

Sudden knowledge strikes me:
I am not the person everyone was waiting for,
but she might be, undine, this slip so whiteblond and blue,
poet for whom all the journals are searching,
teacher, immunologist, secret saint, person
to stand in the way of the long line of tanks.

Or maybe she isn't the answer, either,
pretty child I see once a year and don't know well,
little blond screen onto which I project
the miracle my future needs.

Suddenly lonely, this tacky paradise at the border,
overflown by ravens and the solitary vireo.

HIDDEN SPRING

People have died in these mountains,
the sign at the bottom warned,
do not attempt a trail
beyond your capacity.

After an hour's climb I reached
the old sanatorium, and panted
at the door of those rooms now choked
with thistle and prickly pear,
where the sick had drunk their milk
and slept on cold porches, forbidden
even the small exertion of brushing their hair.

I won't scratch my name into these walls,
as others have done,
                                but my voice, yes,
I would like to throw that
onto these cliffs, to hear it
come back, from where I see
reflections of some pool,
reachable or not,
I don't yet know.

ON BEING CALLED TO PRAYER
WHILE COOKING DINNER FOR FORTY

When the heavens and the earth
are snapped away like a painted shade,
and every creature called to account,
please forgive me my head
full of chickpeas, garlic and parsley.
I am in love with the lemon
on the counter, and the warmth
of my brother's shoulder distracted me
when we stood to pray.
The imam takes us over
for the first prostration,
but I keep one ear cocked
for the cry of the kitchen timer,
thrilled to realize today's cornbread
might become tomorrow's stuffing.
This thrift may buy me ten warm minutes
in bed tomorrow, before the singer
climbs the minaret in the dark
to wake me again to the work
of thought, word, deed.
I have so little time to finish;
only I know how to turn the dish, so the first taste
makes my brother's eyes open wide—
forgive me, this pleasure
seems more urgent than the prayer—
too late to take refuge in You

from the inextricable mischief
of every thing You made,
eggs, milk, cinnamon, kisses, sleep.

HOW THE AGE OF IRON
TURNED TO GOLD

My death makes her way to me
carrying green leaves.

I hear my prayer coming
behind illness, romantic noise,

urgent telephone messages,
alchemical lab results,

like a brook weaving
through thicket.

Water knows the way,
it isn't lost.

My teacher comes to me
by the western gates,

her eyes gone violet
as the peal of a bell

as she bends to gather
all her tender puppies by the neck.

INSTANT COFFEE

When every winged thing
was falling for sweetness
        in my cup,
in the last dregs of light
at the end of a sunset dock,
        I gave up
and poured it in the lake,
and watched that cloud of cream
        expand and hold
an instant in the dark water,
before summer knelt
        into the cold,
dispersing her bright crystals.

EVERY NIGHT

One second before I click off
the light beside the bed
I shut my eyes, to pretend I choose
in which dark I'll sleep.

NOTES & ACKNOWLEDGMENTS

The last line of "How Is It Sometimes" borrows the title of Martha Rhodes' poem "Oh, Luminous" from *Perfect Disappearance*, New Issues, 2000.

The Arabic word *Bismillah*, which occurs in "Baba" and "Prayer at the Gym," means "In the Name of God (Allah)" and is the first word of any Muslim prayer.

The book of poems referred to in "Finding Paul Monette, Losing Him," is *Love Alone: Eighteen Elegies for Rog* by Paul Monette, St. Martin's Press, 1988.

The Latin title *"Consummatum Est"* translates "It is finished," the last words of Jesus, recorded in John 19:30.

The Latin title *"Apologia pro Vita Sua"* translates "Defense of His Life," the title of Cardinal Newman's 1864 spiritual autobiography.

The epigraph to "Fountain of Blood" translates: "The great slender fountains among the marbles"; it is from *"Claire de Lune"* by Paul Verlaine, set to music by both Gabriel Fauré and Claude Debussy.

The title of "Beautiful Orphans" was suggested by Thomas Lux's phrase "beautiful, enigmatic orphans" in his

essay "Not-So-Automatic Automatic-Writing Exercise" in
The Practice of Poetry: Writing Exercises from Poets Who Teach, ed.
Robin Behn & Chase Twichell, HarperCollins, 1992.

The last stanza of "Beautiful Orphans" alludes to Basho's
haiku "Deep autumn— / my neighbor, / how does he live, I
wonder?" *The Essential Haiku: Versions of Basho, Buson, and Issa*, Es-
sential Poets, Vol. 20, translated by Robert Hass, The Ecco
Press, 1994.

*

I am grateful to the journals and anthologies in which ver-
sions of these poems have appeared previously:

American Letters & Commentary: "Your Own Stone"
Art & Understanding: "Rune for Michael, Sick and Far Away"
Barrow Street: "After a Move"
Bay Windows: "Consummatum Est," "Harm Reduction"
Beloit Poetry Journal: "Finding Paul Monette, Losing Him,"
        "After a Long Time Away"
Big City Lit: "Beautiful Orphans," "On Being Called to Prayer
        While Cooking Dinner for Forty"
Bloom: "Pool"
*The Book of Irish American Poetry from the 18th Century to the
        Present*, University of Notre Dame Press: "How
        the Age of Iron Turned to Gold," "Riddle"
"Young Man Reading Colette on the Train" was pub-
        lished in a limited edition broadside designed &
        letterpress-printed by Ben Rinehart at The Center
        for Book Arts, New York.

drunken boat (www.drunkenboat.com): "Prayer Over Dust,"
    "After a Long Time Away"
88: A Journal of Contemporary American Poetry: "To a Variegated
    Begonia"
Four Way Reader #2, Four Way Books: "Riddle," "Finding
    Paul Monette, Losing Him," "Baba," "How the Age
    of Iron Turned to Gold," "After a Long Time Away"
Heliotrope: "Riddle"
The Marlboro Review: "Sweet for All Souls'," "Note to the New
    Owner"
Poetry Daily (www.poems.com): "On Being Called to Prayer
    While Cooking Dinner for Forty"
Puerto del Sol: "Now He"
Rattapallax: "Last Watch," "Young Man Reading Colette on
    the Train"
The Virginia Quarterly Review: "Baba," "How the Age of Iron
    Turned to Gold," "On Being Called to Prayer While
    Cooking Dinner for Forty"
Yale Review: "Instant Coffee"

✳

"Prayer at the Opera" is for Tom Lee; "Prayer After Refusing
to Pray" is for Richard Testa and Francine Friedman; "I Am
Sleeping Where You Died" for Steven and Lotte Simmons;
and "Projection" for the Priestley family: Karli, Marshal,
Sarah, and Tony.

Thanks and more than thanks, to my partner Stephen
Miller, for appearing in time; to my mother Dorothy Best,
whose love of poetry inspired love; and to teachers and

friends Martha Rhodes, Roger Fanning, Joan Aleshire, Carl Dennis, Ellen Bryant Voigt, Peter Turchi, Kevin McIlvoy, J. D. McClatchy, Amy Grimm, D. Nurkse, Frazier Russell, Ellen Dudley, Daniel Tobin, Adrian Blevins, Gary Lilley, Amelia Cox, Robert Thomas, Randall Couch, Rynn Williams, Tracy Hyland, Angela Rydell, Willa Rabinovitch, Sirriya Din, Clifford Browder, Dinah Stevenson, Richard Pierce, Francine Friedman, and Maury Cohen.

I'm grateful to Friends of Writers, Inc. for the Larry Levis Scholarship; to the MFA Program for Writers at Warren Wilson College, for the MFA Scholarship; and to the PEN Fund for Writers and Editors with AIDS for grants in 2000 and 2001.

CPSIA information can be obtained
at www.ICGtesting.com
Printed in the USA
LVOW12s0742231216

518550LV00002B/8/P

9 781931 337069

HEAVY GRACE

▼　▼　▼　▼　▼　▼　▼　▼　▼　▼

Books by Robert Cording

Life-list (1987)

What Binds Us To This World (1991)

HEAVY
·▼·▼·▼·▼·
GRACE

Poems by

ROBERT CORDING

Alice James Books
Farmington, Maine

Library of Congress Cataloging-in-Publication Data

Cording, Robert.
    Heavy grace / Robert Cording.
        p.   cm.
    ISBN 1-882295-09-9
    1. Death—Poetry.   2. Grief—Poetry.   I. Title.
PS3553.05455H43   1996
811'.54—dc20   95-48488
                           CIP

Alice James Books gratefully acknowledges support from the University
of Maine at Farmington and the National Endowment for the Arts.

Heavy Grace was set in Adobe Bembo, a typeface based on the types
used by the Venetian scholar-publisher Aldus Manutius in the printing
of *De Aetna,* written by Pietro Bembo and published in 1495. The
original characters were cut in 1490 by Francesco Griffo who, at Aldus'
request, later cut the first italic types.

Typeset by Wellington Graphics
Design by Lisa Clark
Printing by Thomson-Shore

Alice James Books are published by the Alice James Poetry
Cooperative, Inc. University of Maine at Farmington   98 Main Street
Farmington, Maine 04938

Acknowledgments

Some of the poems first appeared in the following magazines, to whose editors grateful acknowledgment is made:

American Scholar: Crossed Song

Boston Review: September Night; The Mouth of Grief; The Feeder

Cream City Review: For Sarah Winchester

Georgia Review: Instinct

Gettysburg Review: Pop-up Book; Soccoro

Image: After the Funeral; Touch-Me-Not

New England Review: For Rex Brasher, Painter of Birds; Washing the Body

New Virginia Review: Pilgrimage; Glosses

Orion: From the Headland

Poetry: Astapovo; The Cup; Unfinished Sampler

Sewanee Review: Sky-divers; Letting in the Day; Good Friday; White Mountains

Southern Review: AA Meeting; In the Hummingbird Aviary

Tar River Poetry: Cardinal; Zûni Fetish; Prayer

Completion of this manuscript was aided by grants from the Connecticut State Arts Council and the National Endowment for the Arts. I am grateful also to the College of the Holy Cross for its support and encouragement; to Joe Lawrence and Jim Kee and the members of the philosophy reading group; to Don Sheehan and the Frost Place where some of these poems were written; to Bob Deppe and Jeffrey Harrison whose criticism helped shape these poems; to Shirley Adams for her always gracious assistance; and especially to Sydney Lea for his enduring encouragement and support. Finally I offer thanks to my wife, Colleen, whose criticisms and patient reading and rereadings have helped bring these poems to their present state.

—for my parents
And in memory of Eleanor Wenchel

Contents

I wait for the Lord, my soul doth wait
and in his word I do hope.

Psalm 130:5,6

I
▼

Sky-divers

Now, near day's end, they enter our view, at ease
In their wishbones of rope, their red nets of silk

Ballooning above, tracing the summer's liquid breeze
While they fall earthward, unconcerned, their skywalk

Like something we had forgotten for a long time
But now, remembered, turn naturally toward,

And we pause, cars idling at the edge of Route 169,
Each of us, for one reason or another, looking upward,

Alert, hushed, taken up completely by the slow descent
Of our opposites who float above us like an idea

That mocks us and fills us with happiness, such content-
Ment impossible and yet finding form in us here

As we watch them, who are so familiar and so foreign to us,
Until, in the dry fields, they send up footfalls of dust.

Glosses

First light breaking the silence between
the last night sounds and the first

mourning dove's *who, who, who.*

Mist in the trees, sun in the mist
saying itself like a word coming clear.

At once, dispersal: veery and thrush,
white-throat and tanager.

A pair of yellow warblers flaring
from branch to branch, too quick
for my eyes to hold, blinking in the sun.

▼   ▼   ▼

In intervals between passing clouds—
        patches of sunlight, fresh blue
of roadside delphiniums.

        Eight syllables
of a white-throated sparrow come clear

across the field to where I sit, wordless,
paper and pencil in my lap. Eight syllables,

        its syntax
a sentence I know, but have not found
        words for.

▼   ▼   ▼

Speed of a hummingbird's line
in air from wood edge to daylily
and back. Canyons between pines
where light hasn't reached yet;
and a thrush, ventriloquial,
throwing its voice from far back
or near: that story
of a monk who stopped to listen
to a bird's call in the forest.
Returning to the monastery gate,
he found no one who remembered him
he had been gone so long.

▾   ▾   ▾

Just now—a wren trumpets its triplet song.
        The sun pours in. Radiance
in the wingspread of the ruby-throated

        haloing the daylilies'
clean yellow, in their green stems penciled
        on the light—

and then restless waking, the ache
of words incomplete in their praise.

Pilgrimage

They are born for this: to leave
       in the pre-dawn cold. Every year
without knowing, they come to the day
    when they must set out. Now
        again, the machine of the seasons
    turns its gears and geese form

    my attention. Like us, they
        repeat themselves, always
something they are trying to reach,
    something they are trying to get
        away from. Years ago,
    I saw how the summer weekends

    beckoned with their cool nights
        in the mountains, with the wind
blowing in at the shore. Each weekend
    the procession of cars. The transient
        red tinge of brake lights,
    exhaust, watery heat. The sound

    of tires like the sound of waves
        turned once toward the moon,
once toward the earth. Always the promising
    future reassembling itself
        as the past, as the time
    it took for the shuttling pilgrimage.

    Always the nights when I'd hear
        only the tidal migration of passing
cars, a dream I could not wake from,
    nor understand, and yet I knew,
        even as a child, it had to do
    with the ache of something missing.

Reading Emerson

Waking in the night, I rise and pad old boards
That sound my passage in the dark. A mirror

Stops me cold—floats back a shadow-body,
A glinting stooped likeness, here and not here,

Crosshatched by tree branch and moonlight.
We "haunt our lives"—Emerson come back

From my afternoon's reading. Outside,
Five dwarf apple trees shadow the grass.

Two deer have come to eat the windfall.
They draw the shadows around themselves,

Become the trees: quick-muscled limbs
All slow motion, each leaf noise held in

Articulated ears. Now three more inscribe
Themselves on the pearled edge of grass.

Why do I want to clap my hands, whistle, hoot?
Anything to make them move. Their patience tires.

Back in bed, the light's unassignable moment
By moment evolution begins, the sky graying.

"Every look should thrill"—Emerson again,
"Should" a stone his sentence trips over,

A hard reminder of how the world keeps slipping
From attention. Soon the moon will pass

Into the opening mouths of birds whose songs
Will break this darkness. Soon the deer

Will vanish as if they were never here,
As if they are a dream I will wake from

When I rise again, nothing here but shadows
Thrown by the apple trees on which the sun falls.

Soccoro

After a day of driving, of wanting
Our children to see
What we could not show them,
We came to marshes unrimmed by trees
Just as the day was darkening
Heavy-headed clouds that streamed
In the water—plum-blue, purple,
Darker purple—and birds poured
From the air, their wings over us,
Rattling over us
Until we could not hear ourselves
Nor hold in our view
The pivoting, helixed flocks
That formed, shifted, and dissolved,
Uniting and separating, everything
Taking place at the same time.
Shovelers, mallards, coots,
And pintails rocking on the water
Or flying fast and low
Over the water, each of them,
Singly, together, alternately
Calling to its own kind.
Thousands and thousands
Of snow geese—heavy-bodied,
Booming, hammering the air
With such force and unabating
Energy we thought they pushed
A rush of cold wind at us.
We could only stand there,
Shocked by their abundance,
By our sense that skein after skein
Would continue long after
Our parting. And then the slim
Cranes coming in fours and fives,
Long necks extended, a horizon

Of Chinese brush strokes
As they flicked their wings
Upward just once, then glided in.
The children ran along the banks,
Waving their arms, shouting.
They leaped in the air, then fell,
And, in time, just sat there,
Putting their hands over their ears
As the birds kept coming in.
No one spoke as we drove from
The towering din of those birds
Toward Soccoro, the dark expanding
On both sides of the highway,
A flooding dark, unbroken
Except for the single lights
Of house trailers scattered here
And there like boats at sea.

Pop-up Book

Here the world,
Even in plain view, is chameleon
Colored, a face inside the face

Of thick-moving grass,
Of branch and leaf. Open a door
High in a palm

And a pair of ringdoves coo
A doleful love.
Pull a tab and a panther

In the grass springs forward
In pursuit. A deer
Looks back at the sea

Of parted savannah grass
As if it needs another moment
To consider the moment

Already passed.
Don't be afraid, my son says,
Unfolding the snake again

From under its bush.
I can't keep from seeing
Lessons—the undivided attention

Of a great blue heron
Or, free of uncertainty,
The light stride of a gallinule

As it places one foot
After another, on nothing
But water, nothing to bolster

Its confidence
But the sheer delight
Of being there, walking

Just inches out of reach
Of the rising drawbridge
Mouth of an alligator.

One after another
My son goes on opening
The Advent-calendar doors,

Pleased with this world
Of one-thing-behind-another,
With the gaudy excess of it all.

Look, he says, and *look*
And the water teems
With crappie and gar and bass,

The leafy canopy
Of trees releases great egrets
And wood storks, becomes

The dark wings of anhingas
Held out to the sun.
On every page there is a world

Waiting to assume its shapes—
Now a tree frog emerging
From a tree, now a skink,

And, sliding from shadow
To shadow,
The tiny mosquito fish

To remind us of how little
We see of what is always here,
Passing under our noses.

I try to keep pace
With my son, dizzied by
One improbable world

Giving way to another,
Page after page,
Until we reach The End.

The Feeder

The lilacs soaked up rain and light and let go
Of all their lavish odors in one sweet surge.

The poppies aimed at the sun and opened and
Their globes of hinged petals, windstruck, burst

Into flames, and raced like a grass fire across
The new greens. And all in the time it took

(as storm clouds passed over at their own grave pace)
For the day to darken and come to light again.

And all the while, finches and jays, grosbeaks
And juncos, a pair of cardinals and a nuthatch came

And went at the feeder, in and out of my son's sight
Who pointed and waved and stamped with joy and speech:

Bird, Bird. Bye bird. Bird. In my son's eyes,
I saw a world where loss was only a clearing away

For what comes next: a succession of cardinal reds,
Brief goldfinch yellows, greens and blues sharpened

By the windy light. A world always there, always
Going away. My fearful life half over, I saw my son

Find words inside his mouth for the sudden world
He lived in, a world senseless with beauty, undeniable.

Instinct

Big, baggy clouds and a small breeze,
    custodial, going over and over
      the fields with a whisk broom's
resolute, quick strokes. With an ant's devotion
    it carried off bits and pieces
of old newspaper, last year's leaves, husks and
    shells of winter's detritus.

Everywhere the natal tinge of April:
    in the blushing red-tipped maples,
      in the willows' delicate yellow,
in the fields' patchy first greens (where snow
    lay a week ago). Nothing linear
in this plot—repetitive, demanding, April's
    childish light surges in

and again I find myself
    walking toward the river.
      Strange to be drawn so,
year after year, by such mindless resurrections,
    meaningless some would say
when the earth itself is no longer certain
    of abiding. Helpless,

it seems, to change my migratory route,
    I walk toward the river's
      line of oaks, their leaves
still clenched, though the branches shine
    and shiver as if in premonition.
Back home, the phoebes, oddly human, inhabit
    the small, livable space

above the downspout (I've found
    what may be my own hair
      lining their woven nests).

Here the redwings fuss for attention,
    raising tricolor flags.
Near the river, I flush a killdeer and watch
    its deliberate solicitude.

It flutters, it drags one wing,
    then another. It refuses to fly
        off, staking its claim
to an invisible ring of near-mathematical
    precision around the hidden
nest. Devotion? Mere instinct? Young,
    full of myself

and undergraduate knowledge,
    I used to say depth of feeling
        depends on consciousness.
But years and one failed marriage past,
    I held my just-born son,
bloody still, to my lips—and stepped beyond
    the threshold of thought,

the doors of my heart unhinged.
    I would have laid down my life
        for this seconds-old child
I didn't know. I cannot ignore these times
    when my body takes the lead,
and I arrive at these greenish loops of water
    where a heron lifts and

extends one foot so hypnotically time
    seems without meaning and then,
        so quickly only my senses follow,
strikes through its reflection and raises,
    from the river's understory,
a fish, quivering now like something essential
    the mind comes back to.

II

▼

The Mouth of Grief

I remember how we stood there,
In that poorly lit church in Arezzo, straining
With binoculars to see *The Legend,* half worn away.

All afternoon we studied how Francesca added one scene
To the one before until it told the story

Of the True Cross,
Each fresco a signpost pointing the way
Of a past made and corrected and made again,

Without end, as though we were always bound
To discover our innocence was already marked.

We kept coming back to an old Adam
Staggering under the weight of his being.

Even after he has been laid down,
His children cannot understand their father's implacable gaze.

Unimaginable. Unimaginable, that first death
Until Seth, gone for oil of mercy, returns with a branch
From the Tree of Knowledge.

Until that one child finds her mouth opened
Against the silence of a face turned away.

From her mouth,
Those first wild involuntary words must enter
The stricken landscape

No one has ever finished restoring,
Their deep syntax of grief

Something we must have understood even before
We could speak it.

Hands

Generous tears filled Gabriel's eyes. He had
never felt like that himself . . . but he knew
that such a feeling must be love.

James Joyce, *The Dead*

You saw nothing but a face you could not recognize.
Your closest friend's: the re-creation of an undertaker

Working from photographs. There was no trace
Of him. Only you, standing above him,

Your heart closing like a fist. You beat him
With both your hands. But those dull thuds,

That crazed drumming, spoke only of rage
And self-sorrow. Nineteen, you swore never again

Would you love too much. Outside the funeral home,
Flashes of heat lightning, but no rain.

▼   ▼   ▼

On the rocks in the canyon of the Río Pinturas,
The first people printed their hands,

Each an absence in a circle of sprayed ocher.
All over the rocks, hands raised up, arched

Like wings, as if in some ritual people counted on;
As if those images, printed over and over again,

Could ratify their presence and help them believe
The heart's knot of fear might be untied

As mysteriously as dry streambeds are filled
Suddenly with water from an unseen rain.

▼　▼　▼

Tuscany, the wind driving across the fields
Stitched with grapevines, picking up speed,

Entering as unbearable music, each crack
In the stone monastery a pitch pipe.

A shrine there, where a young Francis kneeled
And prayed and discovered a blessing in going naked.

You sat like Jonah caged in the whale, lit
An electric candle that shadowed the smooth stone

Like the birds you made for your fears as a child,
Your two hands standing in for wings.

▼　▼　▼

In her Hiroshima drawing, the artist has drawn
A hand lifted up, each finger burning at its tip.

There is no forgetting the white flash of wind
And heat, the schoolhouse of dead children

Crouched in rows. This hand asks to be loved
Most as it burns away. The drawing is a pledge,

As if the artist had sworn: I will remain here
With you. I will raise my family, keeping your death

Among us. Her drawing asks for belief
In the impossible: from ashen imaginings, a firebird.

▾   ▾   ▾

At the hospital those last days, the two of them
Spending the end as they spent their sixty

Odd years together: in sudden anger, in sadness, in need.
Yet there were moments: "Are you tired"?

The daughter asked. "Are *you*"? the answer snapped back.
"Yes," the daughter replied, and this once did not talk

About what had gone undone or ask what this or that
Doctor had said. She simply rested her hand

On her mother's hand as if they were exchanging
Sufferings. The simplest of gestures.

▾   ▾   ▾

Like Gabriel's who, after his posturings collapsed,
Went to his wife and, asking nothing, touched

His hand to her hair as she slept. In that touch
Something in his heart that had been waiting

All along to reveal itself, burned through
And fell from him, in tears. It spoke the presence

Of the dead, the words
You have held inside for years, but say now,

Renewing the pain that is the only form
Of passage between the living and the dead.

Astapovo

In his last years, Tolstoy believed
In a dreamed-of innocence and tried
To unburden himself of property,
Sacrifice his art to every good cause.

Each day's work never lightened
A weight he could not explain. Always
A rush of words coupling in his head
For a mass of details that would not

Add up. At the end he dressed himself
In peasant clothes (though rubles weighted
His pockets) to slip from his house,
Lived in since a child, to slip from

His wife of forty-eight years.
He got as far as Astapovo, a few stops
On the railway, a few miles into
The country. There he collapsed.

There a stranger's bed soon surrounded
By disciples who waited for what
He could tell them of another world.
He told a son, "I am always composing,

I cannot go to sleep." His children
Waited and his wife who remembered
How he once entered one peasant
Woman after another trying to leave

Himself. Remembered how all these
Years he could not wash them from himself.
He remained in Astapovo, a newsreel
Camera at the window. All he could do

Was lie there, a wet sleety snow
Ticking at the window where faces,
Half-shadowed, half-lit by the little
Orange flames of the gas lamps,

Pushed up to the glass and waited
As if for some final explanation,
Something they could read in the words
Forming on his lips, holding him there.

The Cup

What longing you had to be nothing more
Than the light moving
Across the grass like the stateliest ship.
To move into a light you could not glimpse.
How many times in the dark
Too dark to see in, death came to you,
A weightless lover, and unraveled its beautiful oasis
Out of nothing for you.
And each time you must have thought, "It is right
That I go away and not return."

And yet, after the days
Had lost any gleam of welcome,
After sleep had become a battle
To wake to another pain, it took only our voices
To call you back. There we sat, at bedside,
Saying your name.

As though a human voice could dispel the dream
You wanted to become the world,
You stayed. Or as though you had learned
From all those years
Of sitting at dusk with neighbors,
One or two to a stoop, the close houses
Like sunstruck metal giving back the day's heat,
That there is no place else to go.
Or perhaps the cup of unhappiness you drank from
Was not emptied
Until we could say, "You must go now,
Your suffering is too much for us to bear."

After the Funeral

As if some force we did not recognize,
    or did not wish to,
propelled us, we moved through the afternoon,
    driving past the fronts of houses
        and their fenced dry plots

    of grass where sprinklers stammered
        under a fierce sun.
We stood at the grave, we stood in groups
    passing words between us, everything
        we did not say

    staring back in each other's faces.
        We stood there
Waiting for the moment to leave and then
    we turned back to our cars, the sun
        still pressing down

    like a stone, the light washing out
        all color, the glare
so strong we had to shield our eyes,
    or close them. Afterwards we ate
        and drank and grew sleepy.

    We slept as if great difficulties
        had been faced
and overcome, as if there was nothing
    left to do, nothing to pay
        attention to, not even

    the pain we thought we had buried,
        that lived on
inside us and should have made us more
    alive than we'd ever been, focused
        the intractable present.

We slept the indolent sleep
of grief and whiskey,
our bodies' heavy slumber like the sleep
of those guards in Piero's fresco,
each of them abetting

the other, all of them unable to
move or wake
as Christ steps from his stone tomb.
He has crossed all of night to reach
this moment,

his face wild and fierce with his struggle,
the inrush of light
so sudden, of such intensity, surely
the guards must feel its pressure
against their eyelids.

And still they lie there, so near
and yet turned from
that face they were to watch for as the sun
ferries its passing shadows. He must
have known when

they'd retreat into an easier world
and how, once
he'd slipped from their sight, they'd see
him, time and time again, their whole
sleepless lives.

Cardinal

For a week of mornings, the cardinal came
To the window's glassy face and stalled there,
Its tail and wings sculling, its beak and chest
Stuttering against the dead end of glass.
It flew to its image as if it were real,
The window giving back the self the bird
Couldn't reach or get away from. Summer,
Mid-July, one day bound to another by a sun
Like a silver mesmerizing coin, appearing,
Disappearing, hours ticking in a spell of heat.

My Aunt, her cancer jabbing like a fist
In her spine, woke each morning to a face
Gaping back, "Can that be me?" Strapped in
A wheelchair, doubled over, drugged with pain,
She asked, "What did I do to deserve this?"
That last month of her life her voice
And the psalmists I studied filled my head,
All of them vexed, calling out, "O Lord,
Why art thou so far from helping me?"

Inside myself, I looked out at her pain,
At the cardinal caught in its pool of glass.
Once, the cardinal witlessly knocking
At the window, I chased its image with my own.
Startled, it flew off, a tongue of flame.
That July I read the Psalms, then Bonhoeffer
Who found the heart cannot be comforted,
Such comfort requiring we no longer see ourselves.

My Aunt died in pain. Eighty-three years,
A life long enough for her mourners who came
And went easily. The minister ignored
The life lost to speak of the life to come.
I thought of a heaven of seraphs, psalmists

Who burst perpetually into flame as they sing—
The imagining of men who have sensed
What it might be to step clear through
The mirror of themselves and begin, here, now.

Crossed Song

The days slid away in June's longest light,
In Platonic blue skies and greenest grass,
In iris and columbine and the quick yellow
Of daylilies. High in the trees, warblers'
Whispery *this, this, this* as if in counterpoint
To the earthly towhees' *how to be, to be!*
Each day the melody of their songs as I worked.
And then, just like that, I heard her dying words,
I heard them in the towhees' rising notes
With the same clear urgency—*Don't end up like me.*
I remembered how fear crossed her face,
Again and again, like a bird's shadowed wings,
Each of her last days a ghostly reminder.
Eighty-one years she worked to get things done,
One way or another, and then her days were over,
The world she lived in no more hers than it ever was.
And outside all that June, the air's blue light
Greened with pollen, the nine-folded petals
Of iris unfolded and glistened in the sun.

For Rex Brasher, Painter of Birds
IN MEMORY OF ELEANOR WENCHEL

They are gallant children, living the few swift hours
of life with courage rarely attained by mortals.
Rex Brasher, in the introduction
to *Birds and Trees of North America*

I

This shortened day of wind-flickered yellow-oranges and
  golds,
Of the sumac's heart-colored incandescent glow,

Is like a lifetime compressed into a kiss, given
And received by the dying.

A quick-setting sun in the west, a waxing moon in the east.
Already the indelible outline of the invisible

Fullness to come circled on the sky's darkening shimmer.
Instant by instant, everything intensifies—

Phoebes sieve the air for insects on the verge
Of disappearing and a squirrel, all bristling energy,
  fast-forwards

Across the grass's thinning hair. Now the last eye-urging
Petals of bleeding heart and the chrysanthemums'

Muted rusts and yellows sharpening their color
In the deepening light. Now, the sun's softest angle opens

The spruce, edging each blue-green needle, and a flock
Of sparrows release from the branches' dusky cave

Into the sunlight. My mind reels like a psalmist's
Stricken with wonder, beauty and terror, the world and

The otherworldly, gesturing toward a language
Larger than himself. Always that task.

To conceive a figure for these bright clouds of waxwings
    dissolving
Into light. As Brasher tried to do,

Who wanted to paint, from life, the quiver of the kestrel,
The muscled blue arrow of the kingfisher

Pulled straight to its target beneath the distorting
Water. There was no end to it: 12 volumes, 90,000

Hand-colored prints, 3,000 individual birds.
874 more paintings than Audubon.

And twice, each bird translated at last to paper and color,
He knew what he'd painted was less than he'd known.

One thousand watercolors destroyed.
The necessary repetitions of beginning and beginning.

II

All last summer my grandmother died. At the edge
Of her bed, I read her psalms of praise for a world

Ramified without end, which could just as well be nothing.
She descended into sadness and fear. I held her chill

Hands, stroked their onion paper skin. I tried to bring
The world alive in words. Outside the swallows went

On thinking with their wings. They flashed at her window
Like shadows. She wouldn't look out. I kept wanting

What she didn't have and I couldn't give: words
That could turn her suffering to praise. I kept pointing

Away from ourselves, toward the wind's sudden
And unexpected rise into high spirits or a cardinal,

Crowned and fiery, too wild and strange for the world
Of cut-leafed birch. In the nursing home's long hall,

The old, lined up in wheelchairs, could have been souls
In purgatory. Their mottled arms and hands reached out

Whenever a child skipped by. They'd run their hands
Over my son's head, lightly, as if he were a bird

They held once, long ago. They'd speak to him in dove-like
   coos.
Each day my grandmother worried herself into the dark.

All that time I waited for a moment
When, without need, she would look neither forward nor
   back,

But grow alert to the minutest shifts of light outside
Her window. At the end, I held her, I listened

To her last words—*I am,* she whispered—an answer
To my question: *Are you afraid?*

III

He was seen standing for hours in icy water or bent
To the lettering of bird tracks in the mud, his neck bloodied

By mosquitoes. He'd walk miles or sit in one place waiting,
Trying to learn the difference between possibility

And expectation, the birds always in his mind,
Brush strokes and colors struggling to be visible.

Of course most days his paintings were an indictment
Of his dexterity: the bullying mind omitting and deleting

Or annexing whatever it needs. Not painting was worse:
An exclusion, a sadness that made the world disappear.

As if he were here to see the goldfinches' yellow and black
Flight of falls and risings into paint's affirmation.

Or as if his seeing were made possible only by the
   goldfinches'
Elusive riches. Of course each painting was, in time,

A disappointment. Yet whatever heaven he came to know,
He knew while painting, his heart and his hands given

To the task, say, of the twenty different tans and umbers
Of the wood's understory detailed in a grouse's feathers.

Such work took all his life: ninety-one years
That began in the aftermath of the Civil War only to turn

Again and again to ditches of agony where the dialogue
Of God and man came to an end. He turned to birds,

Their 200 million-year-old history. He saw the reptile
In their feet and eyes. And how the reptile climbed

And perched; made jumps from branch to branch.
Then glidings. Then flights. All those years to trust

The emptiness and grandeur of air. Birds:
Their abundance and variation like the world's,

A world which shouldn't be but is and for no reason.

IV

My grandmother's death just days off, the two of us wearied,
One afternoon we gave up hope for anything more

Than the hours we had. We offered each other
Our arms and a kiss. There was nothing else

To do. I can hardly speak of that moment. There was
The taste of her suffering and pain; and the hush of death.

There was the touch of her lips, cold, waxy, wet with spittle
And sweat. There was the darkness that rose up

To this edge of her body and also a sweetness,
As though her soul had come to rest on the crest of her

Breathing. And there was the terrifying peace
Of the dark wordlessness I found there and keep to this day,

The next-to-last of October, half dark, half glitter
Of dissolving sun high in the green–becoming–gold tamaracks.

My children kick a ball across the lawn plumed
With fallen leaves, the taste of imminent frost in their

Open mouths as it is in mine, the coming winter
A bodily knowledge. Under the trees, the pooling body of
  evening

Slides beneath the afternoon like some otherworldly lover.
And the sky's last violet-reds could be the colors

Of dawn on the earth's other side. Everything—
The tamaracks and maples, the spruces and their
  smoke-winged

Sparrows, the painterly sky darkening toward infinity—
Offers itself as a source of awe. Just now,

The more I listen, the more the geese, high overhead,
  anonymous,
Speak their heart-breaking language. I do not understand,

But believe it has something to do with time, each passing
Moment brief as a life, and yet time enough for a life to
  change.

III

▼

Good Friday

Yet dare I almost be glad I do not see
That spectacle of too much weight for me
John Donne, "Good Friday,
1613. Riding Westward"

Drab as the day itself, two phoebes,
One turning its breast against stick-ends
And sharp dry grass, the other dragging
Clumps of dog hair, sheep wool, moss
From under the spruces. A nest,

Michelet said, is a bird's suffering.
All morning they've worked under
The muffled chill March sun,
Their empty bowl, as likely to fall
As not in the winds to come,

Taking shape on the narrow ledge
Above a window. I'd say it's a longing
That emptiness be filled. I think
Such blind urgency must have turned
John Donne that Friday he rode westward,

Some longing for what he could feel
Only as a loss so deep it stunned him
With its absence into words.
And now I find myself turned toward
This day I've so long forgotten,

As if my own longing were being used
To call me. Donne was almost glad
He did not see. He knew why
He wanted to look away, why he could not
Look any further than the grieving

Mary bound by love to love most fully
In those unbearable hours. I cannot
Say what it would mean to watch a God die.
All morning I've felt again the pain
And fear in each breath used up

Those last minutes of your life.
I remember the weight of your head
And the nest I tried to make of my arms.
And I remember how, with no peace
In your eyes, no words in your open mouth,

No signs nor wonder, death shuddered
Its knowledge into you. Just this
Once I kept death in my sight, stayed
To close its fixed and unblinking eyes.
I cannot say if you knew who I was

Or even if the love I felt for you
In those last hours made any difference.
How strange still, those hours I sat
With you. Each time you cried out,
It left a mark in me. Yet the more

I entered the rawness of your pain
The more some strength of love took hold
Of me. Such violence and peace
In those hours. In the end, Donne cried out
For a God strong enough to make him see.

It was the cry of his heart's longing
To turn to love, no matter the cost.
I have heard that cry this morning
As if it came from inside my own body,
As if, again, it needed a voice to speak it.

Unfinished Sampler

In dark Y's two trees divide
Into two branches leafed in green
Thread. Saffron for meadows
Of grass, kingfisher blue
For the stream ambling through
In little stitched x's.

Two black birds, curved like
A child's eyebrows, create a sky.
In tight-worked vermilion letters:
"For my beloved daughter Rachel."
Then the dates of her short life,
Stitched by a single gathering thread

To bring together the beginning
And the end—and yet the whole left
Incomplete. There's a fence
Outlined with enough rambling roses
To scent each summer day,
Though a little more than half

Were left unblossomed. No way
To know why the mother forfeited
The comfort such handiwork affords.
Why her hand, poised to finish
Another rose, was never lowered.
There's no sign of hurry to fill in

The silence between stitches,
No sign of a moment's irreversible
Despair that there was nothing more
To hope for except the design
Her hands could accomplish.
It's as if she had arrived

At a place she knew she must remain.
As if her symmetry-bound summer world
Became, in time, a reminder
Of that other world Eve had to leave,
Her grief never finished, an emptiness
She had to start over in each day.

AA Meeting

One after another they rise in this basement
Of folding chairs, each telling a different story,
Each saying they're all the same.
A woman, close to three hundred pounds,
Tells how she can't go out, can't drive,
But drinks, the first half-bottle
Vomited before the rest will stay down.
I have come to hear my brother,
An invited speaker, who stands up now.
Sober for more than a year, he's come
To recount the past, a story you could hear
In any bar, but his alone, and he
Must tell it, he must go on explaining
How a man is capable of anything, of how,
Even standing in the aftermath, the blood
Running from his wife's mouth, a child
Hanging from his ankles, begging him
To stop, another, shaking, hiding in
The dark of her closet, he could believe
That whatever happened was not his fault.
I can't look up. My brother is weeping.
Why, I can't help but think, would he tell
These things to anyone, to strangers?
Each Christmas he'd dress as Santa Claus
For a local nursing home. His gift-
Satchel emptied, he'd sit there, laughing
That broad laugh of his, taken up
Completely by love that can be so
Uncomplicated and kind. What makes a life
Take this or that turn, take any one
Of a million possible embodiments?
What made me answer my ex-wife's pleas
To tell her who I was with a silence
So cruel she could only scream? My brother
Is saying now that even pain and self-

Loathing become a nest you can lie
Down in. Everyone nods their yes
Of experience, all family here in their
Knowledge of what things come to.
When I look at my brother, who goes on
Unraveling the intricate knot of love's
Cruelty, unashamed in his shame,
Who points to his heart and says,
It begins here, the will to die and the will
To live, says, *I have taken the first step*
Into another life, I begin to cry
Uncontrollably, the way I've cried over
A radio pop song, some clichéd lyric
Pulling tears from a well I thought
I'd safely lidded. My brother says,
The strange thing is, it's not the pain
That's incomprehensible, but my being here
At all. And yes, even the most uncertain of us
Here must feel the presence of someone raised
Just beyond the reach of everything he did,
Someone whose life has been emptied
Before us, and, still hovering in the air,
Seems a gift, the world a sudden richness.
We feel as if we could love everything,
And we pray, make it last, make it last,
Give us the courage to clear a space
So empty in our own lives
We might live in it, from day to day.

For Sarah Winchester

who was told by a medium that the spirits
of the dead killed by the Winchester rifle
would come for her if she did not keep
building a house around herself.

Days like this, when rain falls, hard,
Then doesn't quite fall, but drifts
In rheumy light, beading up,
Then erasing itself on the new windows,

When the dark comes unnaturally early,
This house, scaffolded again, seems
Something that has emerged
Out of my restless imaginings, my need

To build and rebuild it beyond anything
I can explain. Lost in multiplication,
Wasps fabricate their nests
On the old eave boards, no choice

But to trundle slips of papery wood,
Some pressure inside them to shape
Yet another hexagonal room, their world
Accreting one cell at a time.

For 38 years, 365 days a year,
Hammers repeated their temporal thuds,
Power saws keened their high notes
In her head, her thoughts always

On a future that kept rearranging
Itself as the past, each new room
A balm that was short-lived,
Each orphaned by another. I'm certain

47
▼

All she ever wanted was to be at ease.
Now her house is a curiosity,
The familiar gone strange: 500 windows,
Doors that open on walls or forty-foot

Drops. Tourists wander the long halls,
The 130 rooms stretching like the past,
Labyrinthine as the self. I imagine
Her life was like a dream in which she

Saw herself safe and content,
Sitting in a chair of yellow silk
In a room that she could never quite
Envision . . . All day the rain

Has come and gone. It's left the trees
Black as guns. In their leaves
I can almost see those spirits of the dead.
They seem only to want to be admitted,

To say we could raise them
With our power if only we could
Inhabit our lives. Now, at the light
I've turned on, a moth trapped

In the shade taps like someone
At a distant door. Outside, a shapeless
Fog. A white-throated sparrow calls.
Another, equally invisible, answers.

Again, then again, their eight notes
Clearer than I have ever heard them.
They come through the trees, the fog,
The house as if there were no walls.

Letting in the Day

Not yet a month
Since the death of my colleague at 41
And now, again, we're banding together
To eulogize another friend, dead suddenly
At 44. We gather on the steps, shrug
To acknowledge what we share
Is the feel of what's missing,
And go in. A ballroom fitted out
With folding chairs. Music and testimony.

Again our willful turning to our god,
Memory, to bring back what we believe
Death has taken. How simply we want
To let ourselves become ourselves again,
Death's blunt knife sharpening itself
On our fears. How simply we let ourselves
Become our own gods, each of us desirous
Of a self that can say: *Death*
Where is thy sting?

                           Outside, another
Season sloughs off its used-up days.
These are the quick days
Of pussywillow and sudden snow,
The hours sweeping toward daffodil
And forsythia gone by May.
In this rapid intake of light, the pines
Surge and spark, a green merger
Of branches and the sky's scrubbed blue.
Three or four clouds fray to kite-tails,
Plumes of smoke.

                           I think of another sky
That flashed the same immaculate blue
Above a canyon of bone-dry air,

Pottery shards and stone, a red-tailed hawk
Crossing back and forth, trained on
Whatever moved too self-contentedly below.
Trail markers said: The Anasazi flourished
And disappeared between 900 and 1400 A.D.
This stone, Vishnu schist, was here
When the planet cooled. Touch it
And you touch two billion years.
I did, my own name and all
Human numbers nothing to that geology
Of time.

      When my grandmother died,
Her mouth hung open, a gate
Through which her name seemed to pass
Into anonymity. A breath
Of cold sweat still above her lip,
But already she was gone entirely
To my touch, the hand I held—
Loose-fleshed, blued the color
Of forget-me-nots—completely strange,
Her skin unlike anything I could remember.

For months I tried to keep her in words,
Though the more I wrote,
The more she reminded me of nothing
At all, a vacancy unnaming every phrase,
A lightness more terrifying
Than the weight of all I've wanted
To escape.

      And yet at times I feel
A tremor of peace, the completeness
Of her absence seeming to circle
Through me like the freshest air

Breathed in and exhaled.
Then that moment of greeting
Is lost in the thought of erasure,
My own mind face-to-face with its extinction.

Now the school choir finishes.
A moment of silent prayer, of raw thoughts,
Fears spilling over into fumbling coughs,
Into shuffling hands and feet.
I can hear the yearning
Cranked-up bass thumping from dorm windows,
Its pumped-up declaration
Of how large and powerful the young
Find themselves.

                    Or how small,
Panicked even, their music pouring out
Every minute of every day
As if pitted against time. My own fear-
Stunned moment in the canyon comes back
At me: Who is this "I" I've spent
A lifetime holding apart from everything
Too large for its small boundaries?

When I look up, others,
Too, are crying, each of us floating
In the other's eyes.
The huge ballroom windows are letting in
The day, the sky whistles with light,
And, where its blue gulf
Of air meets the windows, the glass boundary
Between us and what lives outside
Our lives, disappears.

Washing the Body

At the end of your life, you are all weight,
Nothing in your body to help lift it at all.
There is only the empty diagram your lines
Of bones and skin make, worn for eighty-one years,
But never again. Hard to believe this body
Charged so through the world—this still,
It seems never to have moved at all, never
To have risen this very morning. A long day
Of pulling yourself upright, letting yourself
lie down. Then it was done. No matter how
Slowly death comes, it arrives all at once.
Now I run a damp cloth across your forehead,
Feel a crease left by a last frown. I remove
Your valuables as the nursing home instructed:
A watch that hasn't stopped, a wedding ring
Inscribed with promises. I don't know what to do
With your hands. Should I fold them over you,
Or lay them, open, at your sides? Lifting one
To my face, I have to hold it in place, cupped
To my ear like a shell. In your eyes,
The radius of light I knew you by glints
Like a mirror in an emptied room. There is
Nothing to see, yet I may never again see
It so clearly. Nothing to wish for, nothing
To will, now there is only this washing to do.

From the Headland

When I stop to look back at the place I fled,
There is only the calmed ocean where,
Just hours ago, the water erupted in dizzying
Zigzags of porgies; and bluefish, all muscle
And hunger, hundreds of them moving as one
Ravenous body, pressing shoreward in sleek,
Razored runs until the water's troughs and
Swells boiled and spilled over and the beach
Lay rubbled with porgies that thrashed
And went still. Their rich and fetid death
Filled the sky with gulls and pipers, terns
And plovers, their din too much for my ears.

Now there is only the silence of the far
Dunes and the river turning in wide bends
Toward the muddy flats, reddened by a sun
Coming slowly to level on the watery horizon.
The low light simmers on the humped backs
Of the shorebirds, on the beached fish
That shimmer like pools the gravid tide
Has left. The dead and the living are
Hard to tell apart from this distance,
The entire ongoing scene seemingly a stillness
Complete in itself, a row of footprints
Already vanishing in the incoming tide.

White Mountains

At times they nested above us,
Hugely fixed in silent considerings,
Shadow lakes pooled along their sides
As rafts of clouds passed across
The sun. At other times, weightless
As breath, chameleon-like,
They could take the color of rain
And vanish behind a scrim of cloud.
Always expected and always strange—
How, staying in exactly the same place
The mountains were continually leaving,
Day after day, the gray rock
At the peaks gradually darkening
To smoky blue, becoming unmoored
In the Chinese-misted drift of evening.
All that summer as we read or turned
From books, as we stood on the porch
Or moved through our daily tasks
Toward each other, they bridged
Our pleasure and our pain. In the end
We came to believe the mountains
Brought us to some acceptance
Of loss—if only that their high,
Indifferent, ceaseless passing away
Became our only home, their shadow
Line of smoke like the smoke
From the dozen houses on Ridge Road
Where, talking in whispers before sleep,
We spoke of what was still to be done,
The day gone by so unaccountably fast.

IV

▼

Prayer

October, the air filmed as if with tears, and time
Stalled between the light-hearted leaf fall of ashes

And the clenched hearts of oak leaves that stay put
Like misery. Twice a week she greets her mother's stone

With flowers, with pictures, once with an unsent letter.
She tells me how she goes on reaching for the phone.

Twice a day for fifty years it carried their quarrel
Of damaged love. Her mother's death was graceless.

A waiting for pills, for her lungs to fill again,
For the suffocating pain of breath and the fear

Of its departure. For some sign of love denied.
Now each skirmish, even the littlest stray remark

Buried under years heavier than stones is held up
For long scrutiny. Each room of this house holds

Their rankling talk, the two of them sworn to opposing
Ways. And all the while their hopes were twinned,

As in those letters of North and South,
Each opposing soldier a river apart, each homesick,

Dreaming of "taking a loved one by the hand before long."
She leans against the window as if it were a palm

Against her cheek. Outside, the lines of vision are longer,
Avenues between the unleafed ashes. The undersides

Of clouds bloom pinks and reds as the sun expands
At the horizon as it must have for John Keats that autumn

After he'd imagined the world's misery as a school
For his soul. After the Civil War, survivors on both sides

Gathered once a year. Together they watched
The ravaged fields turn to grass. Perhaps they knew

The charity of a world large enough to contain their sorrow.
Perhaps peace fills in whatever space can be cleared for it.

Perhaps stone by stone rolled away, we raise our dead.

In the Hummingbird Aviary
SONORA DESERT MUSEUM, TUCSON, ARIZONA

South of here,
Cortés' soldiers also went still
With astonishment
In the great aviaries of Tenochtitlán,
Overpowered by the grace of white egrets,
By the pattern and colors
Of green parrots, vermilion flycatchers,
Coppery-tailed trogons,
Blue-throated and white-eared hummingbirds.

It's said the men never seemed to tire
Of that city where one world met another
In orchards and gardens,
In lime-washed buildings where
Wild birds nested.

And then Cortés wanted it for his own.
Then the war, the orders, the soldiers
Plunging torches
Into the aviaries. Then the burning air,
The massed, hysterical, screeching birds
Pitching themselves
Against the tumbling wings of others, flaring
Even before the flames reached them.

And, once the grace of things was lost,
That chemistry of destruction, that blind urge
To slap fire to every tree, to roses
And bougainvillea, a running dog, a child.
After, the long walk away,
The tedium of days
Made more terrible by memory
Of that world like none they had ever seen.

Here, we find ourselves still lingering,
Moving instinctively
Toward the hummingbirds
As they come up close and back away,
Stitching their colors from flowers to trees.

There are black-chinned
And rufous, Anna's and broad-tailed.
How quiet we've become,
How patiently we sit and stand,
As though at this moment our vilest desires
Could be pinned by such speed and lightness,
Such needlework,
The marvel of these smallest birds

Changing colors
In each minute's change of light
So that we see them again
And again for the first time,
Now emerald, now ruby, now sapphire blue.

Zûni Fetish

This bear, its humped shoulders and backbone
Scribed like the calm rise and fold
Of oldest mountains, its small upswept
Ears and nose tracking some unseen presence,

Was once half-seen in a common local stone,
Then freed, carved to the fetish I hold
And turn back and forth, darken with sweat
And hand-oil, with half-belief's persistence.

If properly fed, the Zûni believe its power
Cannot fail. To them, it's complete devotion
That gives my bear its strength. Half of me

Counsels against such irrational fervor.
But my ravenous bear waits, a relentless vision
Of heavy grace lumbering where I used to be.

Touch-Me-Not

Touch-Me-Not, we call it, as if unnerved

By this dangling flower's
Covenant with the frail, downcurving stem
From which it depends.

As if we cannot find a language
Without our own fears in it.

At the juncture
Of stem and flower, the touch-me-not rocks

In the smallest breath of wind, rocks
And takes in the heavy August sun,
The damp air.

Its flesh-like purse grows more vulnerable.

When we touch the fullness
Of its rondure, the flower gives itself away,

The prodigal seed coming to light at last,
Falling to earth, each like a word
Holding others inside,

A fluent concentrate
Of frail stem and orange flame,

Of petals soft as the skin of the newly born,
Spotted like the hands of the very old.

Kafka: Lilacs

Even yogurt diluted with water is too much
For him. Unable to swallow, he laughs

At the proofs he has been working on—
Hasn't he become his own Hunger Artist?

At arm's reach, a glass of beer, and pills
To numb the pain, both untouched. A clock

Replays the same hours and the sun
Arrives right on schedule, pausing now

At his window. It deepens the new greens
Of a tree where a bird's voice rises and falls,

Then settles at the sill, on which a vase
Of lilacs rests, their odors given out like light.

He thinks of how these last days, dying,
They have gone on drinking with such pleasure.

In the sunlight, their vase of water sparkles
Like a lake he swam in once with his father,

Each wave made light by sun and movement.
Then they drank beer at a cafe by the shore.

A bird kept reinventing its song. Leaves
Flashed white in the breeze off the water

And on the lake, far out, the single wing
Of a sailboat passed beyond an island,

As if from one realm into another.
And the colors—blues and greens, russet-browns

And creams. Tables of food. Cold beer he held
In his mouth and swallowed . . . When a friend

Wakes him, his room is trellised with blue shadows.
He shuts his eyes again, but there is no lake,

No breeze, no boat. There is only this late hour
And the spray of lilacs he opens his eyes to.

Everything is far and near at once, remote
As memory and yet present as these lilacs he takes

His time to relish, grateful for the way they fill
The room so completely with their rank sweetness.

He cannot eat, though when his friend offers
A bowl of strawberries, he breathes in their scent.

He cannot drink, but asks his friend to drink
For him, to wash down the taste of the fruit.

The Bells
CORTONA, ITALY

In the air always
like sunlight or rain, the bells
of fourteen churches ring
the hours of this walled city

assembled from dust
and stones of other cities
lying just below
these streets, our steps echoing

the daily rounds of
buried Etruscans. They ring
as children wake to
the first light and later as

mothers and fathers
eat midday meals with family—
the sound of silver-
ware and plates, of laughter

and inbred anger
falling from windows shuttered
to the sun's heat.
They ring at dusk as lovers

walk hillside paths
and they are ringing when stars
fill windows opened
for a breeze above the beds

of long-married
husbands and wives, who use
     the few hours they have
to lift away the heaviness

     of each other's day.
Through the dust of summer and fall
     of olives blackened
by cold, the bells clear a space

     for whatever comes
next. Everyone has counted them
     one by one by one
adding losses, and yet, when hill-

     sides wade into bloom,
each of us forgives the earth
     that takes what little
we have made and leave behind.

     Neither louder nor
softer for what passes, the bells
     ring and day after
day, dusk-colored pigeons gather

     in the evening's gold
compressing light, and circle
     together as one
body, diamonded for an instant—

     and then they vanish
into the towers where the bells
     are just ending, their
imprint left behind in air.

Raising the Tree

Spirit music, though no melody in the sounds
Of old timbers weighing my house in the wind.
First lights flicker. Outside, December's gray
Gives way to dark and stars scattered like
Trails, but on a scale too large to follow.

Time again to reopen dusty boxes
Of newspaper-wrapped relics passed down
In time to me. Here's Hannah's glass bird,
The last one still unbroken, and some apples,
Hand-blown from Aunt Emma, who was sick

For a short while, and then was gone
From us, as if she had simply vanished.
From another century, a cherub goes on
Blessing, though I can't remember its story,
And Joseph and Mary, wearied from their exodus . . .

My mother's lost voice breaks in, serious
With instruction: "This crèche was Freida's,
Your great-aunt, who married Norman,
A plasterer whose back gave out when he was
Only forty." Stories I am not to forget,

A roll call of births and marriages,
Children and death. Sicknesses we live through
And die of. I open another box.
I know this star. My grandmother's, it topped
The scentless tree she assembled on her TV.

Proud of her thrift, she used only what was
Reusable. Dead now three years,
She's already a story of the past,
Her house torn down for a new two-family
In that small city where we all lived once,

In rows of houses patient as clocks.
I remember those shortened afternoons,
Brief as this day's dusk, when trees were lit
At almost the same time in front windows,
Their wedges of light relieving the winter.

Now, my little ritual for the year's
Darkest day complete, I take in that moment
When the tree, all of a piece, shines here,
Its topmost star glimmering like some ending
To a lost story I keep trying to reinvent.

September Night

The fields were dark already, the night
Smells of the river breathing steadily
Over them. There was a moth-light breeze
In the poplars, in the dry summer grasses,
And a mass of starlings crossed as one
Body toward a strand of pines, vanishing
In the thick-limbed dark. Disembodied,
Their voices rose up, mixed with the drone

Of crickets, cicadas. Out of nowhere
An owl slid into a night so absolute
I could hardly breathe. I stood among stars,
Cold and still, and mountains that weighed
A silence I knew would be my end
And of which everything I loved was made.

Recent Titles from Alice James Books

Alice James Books has been publishing poetry since 1973. One of the few presses in the country that is run collectively, the cooperative selects manuscripts for publication through competitions. New authors become active members of the press, participating in editorial and production activities. The press, which places an emphasis on publishing women poets, was named for Alice James, sister of William and Henry, whose gift for writing was ignored and whose fine journal did not appear until after her death.